1984

Work in America Institute Studies in Productivity

28

HIGHLIGHTS OF THE LITERATURE

Participative Management

by Fred Massarik

Graduate School of Management
University of California at Los Angeles

Published by
PERGAMON PRESS
New York / Oxford / Toronto / Paris / Frankfurt / Sydney

Pergamon Press Offices:

U.S.A.	Pergamon Press Inc., Maxwell House, Fairview Park, Elmsford, New York 10523, U.S.A.
U.K.	Pergamon Press Ltd., Headington Hill Hall, Oxford OX3 0BW, England
CANADA	Pergamon Press Canada Ltd., Suite 104, 150 Consumers Road, Willowdale, Ontario M2J 1P9, Canada
AUSTRALIA	Pergamon Press (Aust.) Pty. Ltd., P.O. Box 544, Potts Point, NSW 2011, Australia
FRANCE	Pergamon Press SARL, 24 rue des Ecoles, 75240 Paris, Cedex 05, France
FEDERAL REPUBLIC OF GERMANY	Pergamon Press GmbH, Hammerweg 6, D-6242 Kronberg/Taunus, Federal Republic of Germany

Library of Congress Cataloging in Publication Data

Massarik, Fred
   Participative management.

   (Highlights of the literature ; 28) (Work in America Institute studies in productivity)
   Includes bibliographies.
   1. Industrial management – Employee participation. I. Title. II. Series.
III. Series: Work in America Institute studies in productivity.
HD5650.M372 1983   658.3′152   83-17321
ISBN 0-08-029509-6

Printed in the United States of America
First Edition

Contents

REVIEW OF THE LITERATURE   1

    Introduction

    What is Participative Management?

    Some Benchmark Contributions

    Why Participation? The Criterion Problem

    Participation and Organization Structure

    Participation and Culture

    The Practice of Participative Management

    Perspective and Implications

ABSTRACTS   13

RECOMMENDED READING   27

ADDITIONAL READING   35

ADDITIONAL READING (INTERNATIONAL)   39

Review of the Literature

Introduction

"Participative management" (PM) has fascinated managers and organization theorists for many years. In common sense terms, there is something highly persuasive in the notion that workers who take part in making decisions concerning various aspects of their jobs should prove to be more satisfied and more productive, thus, in one fell swoop, improving their personal lot in life (or, at least, at work) and at the same time increasing productivity. In spite of this appealing formulation—and it must be said at the outset that it has much merit—matters have turned out to be much more complicated than one might wish. Essentially, the experience with PM, as applied in practical management situations and as the subject of systematic research, gives rise to apparent inconsistencies in results. "Does PM really work and, if so, when?" remain cogent questions. To respond, a number of factors must be considered simultaneously to determine whether one or another version of PM is advisable in specific circumstances.

Indeed, recently, a number of authors (Brownell 1982; Segovis and Bhagat 1981; Dickson 1981) have addressed the issue of untangling the forces that create uncertainty regarding the particular applicability of PM procedures. There is agreement that there is disagreement—that conflicting and ambiguous results abound as experience with PM is reviewed and analyzed. In this connection, Brownell notes a communications gap between academic researchers and practicing managers and concludes that the introduction of PM develops as a two-step process: managers should (1) "carefully consider the organizational and cultural settings, and (2) fashion a design (in PM) for the firm that adequately deals with its setting." Further, he observes that "the responsibility for ensuring the effectiveness of a participative system rests with the management of a vast range of functional areas within the organization."

Segovis and Bhagat view consideration of "participation" as "similar to being given the task of cleaning the Augean stables of Greek folklore," and point out that [PM] "needs to be evaluated on several different types of criteria. . . . humanistic, democratic, and productive efficiency goals have to be made explicit in evaluating [PM's] impact." Dickson, in considering PM as a possible remedy for work alienation, examines the positions of those viewing PM in terms of its "inherent goodness and moral value . . . [and as a means for increasing] employee satisfaction and productivity."

It is clear that, among other variables, the nature of the particular PM program, its setting, and the expected outcomes need to be considered in relevant *interconnection*, rather than by making the simple assumption that PM is inherently "good for all sorts of purposes, stated or implicit." It does not seem appropriate, therefore, for the practicing manager to be either an absolute "advocate" nor an absolute "opponent" of PM. Instead, an analytic approach—perhaps tempered by a mixture of hope and skepticism—may be in order. And it must be recognized that PM is not a single temporary intervention that is likely to yield results that are both immediately recognizable and permanent. More realistically, fully developed PM may be regarded as an expression of a fundamental management philosophy that calls for a *process* of activities—and of changed relationships—at all levels of the organization hierarchy. In view of this complexity, a fundamental rethinking of what PM is and what it may accomplish seems in order. Such reanalysis should help clarify relevant concepts and point toward effective selective application of participatory approaches.

0149-8703/83/00001-40$05.00/0

What Is Participative Management?

The central concept of participative management may be stated as follows:

> Persons at subordinate levels of an organization's hierarchy take part, in varying degrees, in making decisions regarding the organization's and their work jointly with persons at superior levels of the hierarchy.

In other words, PM covers a broad spectrum of possible activities, ranging from highly specific and narrowly delimited inputs by a given worker concerning his or her tasks in discussion with a supervisor, to far-reaching, definitive determination of work objectives and procedures, over long time periods, involving top management.

Dachler and Wilpert (1978) have developed a comprehensive conceptual framework concerning participation in organizations. They consider relevant *contextual boundaries; values, assumptions, and goals; properties*; and *outcomes* of participation. Importantly, they draw our attention to the broad environmental context and to basic values that generate and effectuate programs of participative management—and note that the outcomes appear at individual, group, organizational, and societal levels.

Segovis and Bhagat (1981) observe that "several authors have defined participation in the language of industrial democracy; other authors emphasize that participation is an influence process. . . or power equalization, while still other analyses would include Scanlon Plan and job enrichment programs."

An earlier effort to conceptualize PM (Tannenbaum and Massarik 1950, 1961) defines participation as a managerial device, and focuses attention on the subordinates of managers in enterprise as the participators. With participation in decision making as the core notion, Tannenbaum and Massarik provide a three-step framework, emphasizing rational aspects of this process: "the individual [participator's] awareness of the maximum number of possible behavior alternatives relevant to the decision; the participator's definition of each of these alternatives, determining as many as possible of the consequences related to each alternative; and, finally, the participator's actual choice among alternatives—the making of the decision itself." In practice, however, these steps do not necessarily follow in precise order, and they may involve considerations other than rational choice.

Another critical issue bearing on the nature of a given PM program relates to the balance between subordinate-centered and superior-centered decision making—the extent to which the manager uses authority unilaterally as contrasted with areas of freedom available to subordinates. This matter has been presented with exceptional insight by Tannenbaum and Schmidt (1958, 1973). Of special interest in this work is the "continuum of manager-nonmanager behavior," reviewed in the authors' retrospective commentary, 1973-1958. With eventual recognition of the significance of organizational environmental and societal forces, they specify seven types of relationships between manager and nonmanagers of which the following four are most descriptive of participatory decision making:

- Manager and nonmanagers jointly make a decision, within limits defined by organizational constraints.
- Manager defines limits within which nonmanagers make decisions.
- Manager presents problems, gets inputs from nonmanagers, then decides.
- Manager presents tentative decision, subject to change by manager after nonmanager inputs.

This conundrum of keeping or delegating decision authority is pervasive and has a long history. For instance, we find a remarkable anticipation of Tannenbaum and Schmidt's work in the mid-thirties by Hader and Lindeman (1933), unknown to Tannenbaum and Schmidt until the late seventies. This earlier framework proposed a continuum ranging from acquiescence to another's decision, to integration of decision among superiors and subordinates. Indeed, to understand PM in its present versions, it is useful to examine it in light of a number of "benchmark" contributions, several initially presented some four or more decades ago.

Some Benchmark Contributions

While the issue of "participation" in its most general sense, no doubt, may be traced to classic theories of politics and statecraft—as, for instance, to theories on the participation of citizens in the government of ancient Greece—in more contemporary context, much thought on PM is rooted in the germinal work of Kurt Lewin. In Lewin's writings on "group atmospheres," distinguishing autocratic, laissez faire, and democratic leadership styles, the latter is identified as essentially participatory (Lewin, Lippitt, and White 1939).

Perhaps the most directly visible benchmark contribution in the current sense of PM is the work of Douglas McGregor who, in a line of intellectual development traceable to Lewin, introduced the notion of *Theory X* and *Theory Y* in his *The Human Side of Enterprise* (McGregor 1960). While the much-cited Theory Y, described by McGregor as "the integration of individual and organizational goals," calls for and is linked to PM procedures, McGregor separately addressed the issue of participation and, indeed, provides appropriate reflections, relevant as ever (McGregor 1960, ch. 9):

> Participation is one of the most misunderstood ideas that has emerged from the field of human relations. It is praised by some, condemned by others, and used with considerable success by still others. . . . [effective managers] make successful use of participation, but they don't think of it as a panacea or magic formula. . . . They would flatly refuse to employ participation as a manipulative sales device.

Elsewhere in this book, McGregor considers the significance of one carefully organized systematic approach to PM, the Scanlon Plan (1960, ch. 8). The Scanlon Plan, addressing issues of union-management cooperation, continued upon Scanlon's death in 1956 by Frederick Lesieur and subsequently adapted in many forms, is based on a linking of two approaches:

- Cost-reduction sharing, i.e., the sharing of economic gains that result from improvements in organizational performance.
- Effective participation, providing opportunity for all organization members to contribute ideas and proposals for improvement by means of a series of committees designed for this purpose.

Looking at PM in a more "microscopic" way, Argyris (1957) pointed to the dangers of "pseudo-participation," which, however, is not translated into the kind of climate that facilitates genuine give-and-take.

Quite neglected in much recent theorizing on PM is Gordon W. Allport's significant analysis of "the psychology of participation" (Allport 1945). Allport points out that mere activity—even if it involves discussion of tasks at work—is not necessarily participation in any real sense; rather, authentic participation taps *central* values, calls for the person's ego to be engaged with the issues considered, and constitutes an approach to the *complete person*.

An extensive and well-documented case example of PM is provided by Alfred J. Marrow and his associates in *Management by Participation* (Marrow, Bowers, and Seashore 1967). Comparisons are made between two manufacturers, Harwood and Weldon, the former making wide and effective use of participative methods, while the latter operated in accordance with the conventional authority-obedience system. Eventually, the participative methods that had been well-tested at Harwood were successfully introduced into Weldon. The process involved and the conceptual and practical problems encountered are clearly documented.

The practical orientation of *Management by Participation* was based in important respects on research conducted by the Institute for Social Research at the University of Michigan, and particularly on the work of Rensis Likert. Of special significance is Likert's *New Patterns of Management* (1961). Likert considers four contrasting management systems, which he describes as "exploitive authoritative," "benevolent authoritative," "consultative," and "participative group." The latter is based on motivational forces calling for full use of economic ego and other major motives, as, for example, motivational forces arising from group processes, with attitudes "favorable, cooperative . . . throughout the organization with mutual trust and confidence." It should be noted that Likert's work is not presented as speculative theory, but rather as based on a program of research begun in 1947.

More recently, approaches to PM variously associated with management styles prevalent in Japan have received much attention. Perhaps best known among these is *Theory Z* (Ouchi 1981). Also well known and widely cited is *The Art of Japanese Management* (Pascale and Athos 1981). Ouchi observes (p. 43) that "probably the best-known feature of Japanese organizations is their participative approach to decision-making," and notes (p. 39) that "the basic mechanisms of management control in a Japanese company are so subtle, implicit, and internal that they often appear to an outsider not to exist."

Pascale and Athos examine contrasting management styles in organizations such as Japan's Matsushita and the worldwide conglomerate ITT, incorporating varied approaches to participation. It is clear that underlying cultural considerations, rather than mere techniques, are central if one is to understand the extent to which particular PM methods may prove applicable in one or another organizational and cultural milieu.

Why Participation? The Criterion Problem

Some enthusiastic supporters believe that, like old-time patent medicines, PM is "good for what ails you." This position may be softened by "Well, of course, it all depends," but quickly, no matter what the circumstance, some form of PM is instituted. The rationale may range from misinterpretation of humanistic values to selective attention to *anything* positive that in some fashion might be related to a PM effort. Unfortunately, more than a few organization development practitioners find themselves entangled with this approach, in which patent medicine and participative management become synonymous.

As one examines the issue in perspective, at least two questions popularly recur: Does PM improve productivity? Does PM improve worker satisfaction? A review of research by Locke and Schweiger (1979), characterized by Segovis and Bhagat (1981) as "comprehensive and scholarly" is helpful, but—alas—not definitive. The difficulty rests with the varied study designs, methods, and definitions on which available research is based.

In response to the first question, Locke and Schweiger conclude that, using a broad criterion of productive efficiency, more than half (56 percent) of the studies indicate that there was no difference between instances in which PM was utilized and those in which it was not. Further, for the balance of the studies considered, an even split (22 percent each) appears for those suggesting superior or inferior productivity—quite a fuzzy picture, indeed.

In response to the second question, the situation appears more hopeful: In 60 percent of the studies, measures of satisfaction and/or morale point to superior outcomes. Thirty percent noted no material difference and only 9 percent hint that PM was followed by some decline in satisfaction or morale.

A major compilation of research on leadership (Bass 1981) cites evidence to the effect that PM substantially promotes concurrence in, and acceptance of, decisions reached in the PM context. It also makes reference to additional inquiries, conducted in settings as varied as school administration, air crew operations, and conventional management, and points to positive causal connection between PM and worker satisfaction.

At another level, PM is seen as potentially useful in the reduction of stress and as a possible remedy for work alienation (Dickson 1981). Extensive contributions by Janis on decision making under stress (Janis 1982) have important implications for the relevance of PM as an approach to stress reduction.

Next we turn to some key issues relating to PM as a managerial approach.

Participation and the Individual

Some two decades ago, Vroom (1960, 1964) examined various personality determinants relating to PM and concluded that "the effects of participation in decision-making depend on certain personality characteristics of the participants." He noted that "the evidence suggests that authoritarianism and need for independence interact with participation in determining attitudes toward the job and motivation for effective performance"; and that "practices or methods which are appropriate for dealing with persons with one set of personality characteristics may be entirely inappropriate for others." While subsequent research raises questions as to Vroom's specific findings (Abdel-Halim and Rowland 1976), both research and practical experience generally support the view that the characteristics and dynamics of individual subordinates must be considered in planning any given PM program.

Hill and Schmitt (1977) in subsequent research generally support Vroom and Yetton (1973), noting that while in a series of experiments the *situation* was of considerable importance, well-discernible individual differences in decision-making style were identified.

In an examination of the relative contributions of several individual difference factors to aspects of PM, Steers (1977) found that females generally were more participative than males. Stearns (1981) reviewed the work on two leadership styles: *Alpha* and *Beta*—the former characterized by an analytical, rational, hierarchical, win-lose perspective, and the latter by adaptive, intuitive, and participatory qualities. In typical U.S. settings, as demonstrated in tasks requiring solutions to survival problems, the Beta style is more typically associated with women than men. In Japan, however, it is also appropriately descriptive of males. Stearns suggests that Beta may develop more distinctly in women in certain cultures because of the woman's role as "family negotiator," and observes that some pressures may appear in male-dominated fields that oblige women to adopt Alpha. A prior source (Rosener and Schwartz 1980) suggested the terms Alpha and Beta and developed underlying concepts.

In this context, attention is drawn to the relevance of sex roles to PM, and to personality constellations which, while not exclusive to one or the other sex, are regarded as acceptable if displayed by members of one or the other sex in contrasting culture settings.

The relevance of *expectancies*—as, for instance, regarding the extent to which participation will be followed by concrete action—has been considered by numerous authors. For example, Schuler (1980), in a study of employees at various hierarchy levels in a large manufacturing firm, concludes that participation in managerial decision making is positively related to performance-reward expectancies. On the other hand, role conflict and ambiguity are regarded as detrimental to participation.

The manager concerned with the development of PM systems evidently needs to take into account a variety of personal characteristics and dynamics; aspects of personality structure, such as authoritarianism, desire for structure, sex roles, and expectations concerning the effects of participation, are illustrative. One quickly finds, however, that individual characteristics and dynamics do not exist in isolation, but that they are much intertwined with the organization's structure and climate, and with the broader culture.

Participation and Organization Structure

We must quickly dispose of the issue of centralization versus decentralization. In itself, it does not speak to the matter of participation, although managerial attitudes favoring decentralization may be mildly associated with a favorable view of PM. To the extent that PM calls for face-to-face interaction, small organization units may be desirable for decision-making interaction as such. It is, however, possible to construct such units, even within the framework of organizations that in terms of ultimate decision-making authority are described as centralized. By way of illustration, certain procedures relating to MBO (management by objectives, to be considered below) point to the feasibility of the development of small subentities for specified, if not for all, PM functions.

Perhaps more important than centralization or decentralization as such is the extent to which participative decision making is formally and explicitly built in to the structure of the organization. Nightingale (1981) examined the relationship between "formal" decision-making structure and "informal" supervisory style and their combined effects on various outcomes. He found that both the formal structure and informal supervisory style brought about significant effects. Indeed, participative and supportive supervisory practices tended to occur more typically in formally participative organizations, and organization member outcomes proved to be more positive in these organizations than in the explicitly nonparticipative organization structures. One concludes that organization structure "sets the stage" and helps to establish the climate within which PM efforts are established.

Formally participative organizations involve *redistribution of power* and reflect *value changes* at both management and worker levels (Nightingale 1979). Still, as Mulder and Wilke (1970) noted on the basis of an experimental study, power *equalization* between the "haves" and "have-nots" is not necessarily the outcome of a particular PM approach; indeed, PM may provide the initially more powerful with greater opportunities for using their power in subsequent situations.

Related to the matter of power redistribution is the issue of *ownership*. The ideological and political aspects of PM that relate to ownership of the organization are complex and far exceed this essay's scope. However, one observes that ownership per se does not inevitably yield incremental impact in participation. Long (1981) found that in an electronics firm that converted to partial employee ownership, little change took place in perceived participation at each decision level, in desires for participation and/or in distribution of control and influence. Perhaps, then, it may not be the structure as such, even if it is expressed in direct or partial ownership, that is critical.

More likely, structure facilitates and/or constrains PM, in interaction with other factors. Perhaps of greatest importance is the matter of organization *climate*. For example, Driscoll (1978) points to organization *trust*, as indicated by PM participants' views of decision makers, as a factor of major importance in predicting participants' levels of satisfaction—and perhaps other positive PM outcomes.

The concept of organizational climate also has numerous and complex facets. One observes the substantial interrelationship between climate and other organizational variables (James et al. 1979; Norton 1976). This interactive character is well demonstrated in the James et al. study of contrasting high- and low-technology jobs, which examines the correlates of subordinates' perception of their psychological influence on supervisors' decisions. It is found that the influence of the psychological climate pervasive in the organization is significantly linked to *situational attributes* (such as a supervisor's behavior), *individual characteristics*, and *interactions between person and situation*. Norton points to the relevance of positive views of work environments, on the basis of a study of management-level personnel in a large corporation, and their relationships to explicit and implicit structural variables.

In affecting PM—by creating constraints and/or aids to the PM process—structure, no doubt, plays a role. However, in combination with other factors, including the interacting managers/nonmanagers and the situation, organization climate expressive of management philosophy is highly significant in furthering or impeding (or, for that matter, preventing) the implementation of PM programs.

Participation and Culture

Once again we face issues of definition: the concept "culture" carries many connotations. Nevertheless, there is reasonable agreement that "culture" deals with widely pervasive and generally durable elements that characterize some collection of people (as, for instance, an organization, nation, or broader geographic area) and that it involves both values and beliefs and "ways of doing things." In light of this definition of "culture," it is clear that consideration of culture is relevant for an understanding of *organizations in cultures* and for *the culture of a given organization*. Indeed, every organization evolves its own culture; this culture in turn is influenced by (and influences) the general encompassing culture, which characterizes the country, or broader milieu in which the organization is embedded. Issues of relationships between organizational culture and national culture are among those affecting participative management.

Quite typical of the early 1980s are efforts to transplant PM approaches characteristic of one cultural milieu into another, particularly those of Japan to the United States. In simplest form, the rationale—a somewhat defective syllogism—goes like this:

"Japan has unusually high levels of productivity."

"U.S. productivity has been slipping."

"We used to think that the Japanese imitate us."

"Now the time is right for us to imitate the Japanese."

"This will improve U.S. productivity."

We have previously referred to two widely known books (Ouchi 1981; Pascale and Athos 1981) that, for better or worse, have been identified with this line of reasoning. A briefer statement in this regard (Ouchi 4 May 1981), describing the Type Z organization as having attributes of both Japanese styles (Type J) and American styles (Type A), proposes that management styles are not necessarily culture bound and that there are large companies in the United States which can be said to be Type Z organizations.

An example of an adaptation of Japanese management approaches, including various PM procedures, is reported by Main (1981), with reference to Westinghouse's cultural revolution. Predictably, the experiment at a division of Westinghouse began in the cause of productivity increase, by adaptation of a Theory Z-type system. Participative management teams were set up, and many decisions were achieved by consensus. Other devices, such as quality circles (a procedure whose consideration is beyond this paper's bounds), were implemented. Main reports that while most managers became "consensus enthusiasts," blue-collar reaction varied considerably.

A cautionary note is sounded by Moran (1979), who notes that, while some Japanese techniques can be productively applied in the United States, many Japanese management practices, given the paternalistic character of Japan's industry, cannot be transferred to this country. One needs to consider, therefore, the character of the specific PM philosophy and program and its fit with the enveloping culture setting.

At the other end of the world, participative techniques find varied application in Europe under the heading "industrial democracy," and "humanizing the world of work." A helpful overview of these developments is provided by Geiger's review of the movement for industrial democracy in Western Europe (Geiger 1979). He notes that various programs of codetermination, involving worker participation in management, are prescribed in the laws of various European countries, among these West Germany, Sweden, and the Netherlands. Thus, the framework for PM in the cultural environments indicated functions in the context of legal prescription, rather than through voluntary local management choice. Participation in decision making in these settings variously occurs at widely disparate levels—on the shop floor, in the board room, and at stockholders' meetings.

Empirical studies of worker participation in Europe abound. Bartolke and his associates (1982) studied workers' participation and the distribution of control in 10 West German companies and conclude that "the distribution of control was more egalitarian and/or that it implied a greater total amount of control in the more participative compared to the less participative companies." Illustrative of work elsewhere are studies by Kavcic and Tannenbaum in Yugoslavia (1981) and Norrgren in Sweden (1981a,b).

In these European settings, no less than in the United States, PM fails to be a simple one-dimensional procedure. The research cited illuminates a variety of aspects of a complex process, unfolding in a multiplicity of situations. Here, one is inclined to wonder whether systematic differences in PM appear in socialist vs. capitalist countries? An extensive study in fifteen countries (Jacob and Ahn 1979) examined why some workers in these countries actively seek to participate in decision making while others remain apathetic. It was found that few differences appeared between socialist and capitalist countries; what seemed to matter was whether an individual worker felt that the specific work system provided him or her with sufficient clout in satisfactorily affecting working conditions. This finding is consistent with

7

the view that, while aspects of culture may play a role in the general applicability of PM programs, a core consideration that cuts across cultural boundaries relates to the individual worker's desire to shape relevant aspects of personal occupational destiny.

In India, too, worker participation is practiced in various enterprises and, indeed, is enshrined in the Indian constitution, which provides for "the participation of workers in the management of undertakings, establishments or other organizations engaged in an industry" (Raghavan 1978). Having considered the impact of individuals, organization structures, and cultures on PM, we now turn to some practical PM applications.

The Practice of Participative Management

It is evident that there is not a single participative management—that there is no "standard model" that can be instituted or removed at will. Over many years, a great variety of PM techniques, methods, procedures, and philosophies have been devised, named, and promulgated. In every instance, the amount of commentary, opinion, and research is voluminous. In this reconsideration of PM, we wish only to draw attention briefly to several of the best-known practices, to provide the reader with some guidelines for further inquiry.

One of the oldest systematic PM practices is the *Scanlon Plan*. As noted earlier (McGregor 1960, ch. 8), the Scanlon Plan is based on a formal program of participation, together with a program of financial incentives. White (1979) investigated the factors that seemed to distinguish more successful from less successful Scanlon Plan applications. He found that success was significantly associated with the following: (1) supportive attitudes toward the plan by management, and particularly by the CEO; (2) the extent to which participation in decision making was reported by the employees; and (3) the number of years that the plan had been in operation. However, apparent success did not appear to be related to company size. Accordingly, the Scanlon Plan may be seen to have desired impact if it is well supported and positively perceived by members at various levels of the organization, and if it is given sufficient time to take root in the organization's culture.

Proposed and interpreted by Drucker and others in the 1960s, *management by objectives* (MBO) has had a varied history of vogue and disuse, of success and failure. In essence, MBO calls for a process of deliberation between superiors and subordinates (typically on an annual basis) regarding goals/objectives to be achieved and resources to be allocated for this purpose.

In the context of a prolific literature on MBO (a literature requiring consideration on its own merits), we may point to several current clarifications and elaborations of MBO practice.

It has become increasingly clear, as pointed out by McConkie (1979), that the process of setting goals and objectives must take realistic account of the framework of time and the priority in which it proceeds. The statement of goals and objectives needs to be specific and operational, and periodic appraisal and review—including options for resetting goals and objectives and resources—need to be provided. This is the case, especially in rapidly changing economic and technological environments. In terms of PM, such response to change calls for flexible and responsive procedures.

MBO demands substantial know-how by all participants. Expertise is required both at the technical level and at the level of interpersonal process. Aplin and his associates (1979) have pointed to a concept of "tough-minded management by objectives" as an approach, with the caveat that managers should not attribute to the participating subordinates managerial skills and sophistication levels that, in fact, are not available.

A number of observers of the MBO scene have proposed *group or team approaches* (Likert and Fisher 1977; Weihrich 1979). Here, teams or work groups, rather than individuals, are engaged in the process of setting goals and objectives, and in participating in other MBO activities. Likert and his colleagues in proposing MBGO—management by group objectives— express the view that such shared effort reduces the probability that individuals will seek to achieve their own personal objectives at the expense of others. In the same spirit, Weihrich advocates TAMBO—a team approach to MBO—calling for team procedures in objective setting, action planning, plan implementation and control, and appraisal, with systematic consideration of organizational climate, structure, technology, and the interpersonal system.

Finally, in this connection, we may note the use of *participative budgeting management by objectives* as part of an integrated approach to corporate planning and budgeting (Lin 1979). In this procedure, the budgeting elements associated with overall planning functions are specifically implemented by means of an MBO approach.

Still another practice, again with a considerable knowledge base of its own, is *matrix management*. Especially as popularized in applications in high-technology industries, matrix management calls for the development of project teams to complete specified program assignments. For this purpose, coordinated effort by multidisciplinary teams is instituted; the team members may be drawn from different functional areas and from varied hierarchy levels (Greiner and Schein 1981). By its very nature, matrix organization calls for participatory effort in the making of decisions and, normally when a matrix is instituted in the context of conventional organization forms, behavioral changes by all participants (Kolodny 1981). With this in mind, the latter author notes that a matrix system is capable of processing different types of information (particularly those required in complex problem solving) efficiently, and that formal hierarchic levels can be transcended so that all relevant data and skills may be focused on the task at hand. To bring this about effectively, substantial time and effort by managers at all levels and by all participants in the matrix system are required.

Matrix organization is seen as providing competitive advantages, especially when rapid technological change, product variety, and complex technical and software problems are addressed (Wright 1980), and as product innovation is required (Kolodny 1977).

Given the fact that matrix organization involves a web of interpersonal and technological factors, many of them at odds with conventional corporate forms, it is not surprising that a variety of special, and sometimes unique, obstacles must be overcome. Davis and Lawrence (1978) have pointed out that dual chains of command can cause excessive or inadequate controls, and that the risks of anarchy, power struggle, inappropriate reliance on group process, and the like are present, particularly in business decline and organizational stress (Davis and Lawrence 1978).

The nature of interpersonal problems associated with matrix is variously treated by Wolff (1980), and by Lawrence, Kolodny, and Davis (1977). With matrix organization requiring that participants "work together" and making demands on the organization's technical capacities, the need for specially designed training programs and team building is widely recognized.

Balanced assessments of positive and negative aspects of matrix management are provided by Rowen, Howell, and Gigliotti (1980) and by Wright (1979), while Peters (1979) proposes approaches extending beyond matrix organization. He suggests four guiding principles: to find better ways for managing the team functions (as contrasted with creative functions); to find ways for avoiding the special difficulties to which matrix is heir; to be responsive to the limitations due to the organization's past forms and history; and to remain involved on a continuing basis in a process of change and perpetual reorganization.

Among other major PM practice modes are *Consensus Management* and *Consent Management*. The former, rooted at least in part in Quaker consensus (Drake 1974), has found application in long-range corporate planning (Naor 1978), and in general management practice (Dowling 1977). Consensus planning is seen as calling for a broad-gauge participatory approach, extending the consensual process across several corporate levels; eventually an overall consensus long-range plan may be developed by the total planning group.

Dowling (1977) emphasizes that consensus management requires top-level corporate support, and that a consultant is needed to maintain consensus management on a continuing basis, as in the Graphic Controls Corporation example cited.

Handy (1977), in consideration of management by consent, examines new problems that may arise when authority for agreement is granted to workers and asserts that management still maintains final authority in consent decision making. It is evident that, in terms of the theory underlying PM, both philosophic and procedural issues must be continually considered if the chosen practice is to function appropriately in a given organization setting.

In conclusion, we turn to an overview of participative management and to a consideration of possible steps in future application.

Perspective and Implications

The discussion so far has noted the interlocking issues that bear on PM as a concept and as a mode of managerial practice. It is useful to recall that while PM often is instituted as a "program," or even as an "OD intervention," especially as a specific short-term issue is addressed, PM is fundamentally a reflection of a *human resources policy* (Koch and Fox 1978; Applebaum 1979). In turn, such policy implements a management philosophy, as may be reflected at a given time by the incumbent CEO and by other central policy-forming individuals or entities, formal or informal.

We have previously noted the importance of organization climate and compatibility of the PM approach with the organization as a whole. Similarly, a given PM program intended to affect only a part of a larger organization system (generally a risky arrangement) needs to consider the impact as the unit in which PM is instituted interacts with other units, some possibly characterized by significantly different organizational climates.

What conditions facilitate participatory-democratic organization forms? Rothschild-Whitt (1976) has carefully addressed this topic in an analysis of "alternative institutions." While such institutions (free clinics, for example) have unique aspects, some of the facilitating conditions cited have wider relevance. These consist of: (1) a "transitory orientation" (the system has a limited life span and continuity depends on fulfilling its central goals); (2) a supportive professional base (interpretable in the context of other organizations as a sophisticated and able core group that wants to maintain a participatory mode); (3) an orientation toward mutual criticism and self-criticism (involving sanctioned ways of realistically assessing current strengths and weaknesses); and (4) limits to size and alternative growth patterns (providing for "face-to-face, personal relationships and direct-democratic forms," with self-limitation approaches if a potentially excessive size is approached). Development of "networks" may provide facilitating linkages among relatively small, highly participatory autonomous units.

As Lowin (1968) has noted, many approaches to organizational participative decision making need to take account of equilibrium and social change. Such concerns with homeostasis, to keep things going at some desired level of activity, necessarily need to consider the dynamics of *individual motivation* and the blending of such motivations, or conflict with the larger organizational system, its climate, and the society's culture.

At best, as Bistline (1980) has enumerated, PM may be able to provide a veritable cornucopia of positive outcomes: better decisions; higher productivity; improved morale and job satisfaction; reduced tardiness, turnover, and absenteeism; better communication; and more effective resolution of conflict. Bistline correctly observes that some PM systems may be as simple as a straightforward *suggestion program*, while others may call for radical change in managerial concept and structure. Participation is like the proverbial little girl with a curl in the middle of her forehead: "When she was good, she was very, very good, but when she was bad, she was horrid."

While a more systematic approach (including a clearly defined research procedure, in preparation by author*) to determine the applicability of a given PM program may be required, the following guide questions serve to set the tone:

---

* Inquiries to F. Massarik, c/o BSRA, 4320 Cedarhurst Circ., Los Angeles, CA 90027.

1. What motivates introduction of the PM program? Specifically, *who* (and for *what* personal and organizational reasons) wants to achieve what by means of the PM effort?

2. How compatible is the proposed PM program with the organization's social and economic climate, as manifested by its history, core values, and typical "ways of doing things?"

3. Is an articulate philosophy in place—by top management and other key decision makers—to establish a basis for the PM program?

4. What are the probabilities that the PM program will be supported by nonmanagerial key individuals and groups, including unions?

5. What are the probable principal resistances and constraints (technology included) encountered in the introduction and development of the PM program? What are the principle facilitating forces?

6. Exactly *who* is to participate with *whom*, in the making of *what* decisions?

7. What are the *real* limits of authority and delegation (superiors' determination vs. sub-ordinates' freedom) characterizing the PM program?

8. What are the specific mechanics (e.g., committee meetings, team efforts, written procedures, and so on) required in PM program implementation?

9. What time period is available for introduction of the PM program, and how much time is to elapse before results are expected? (Since, events in organizations have many simultaneous causes, how much assurance is required that given results are traceable *specifically* to PM?)

10. What are the priorities among the many criteria of success (and the numerous risks of failure) that must be considered as the PM program is instituted, implemented, and appraised?

A comprehensive and a suitably diagnostic mode of approach is in order as PM—with all its history—is reconsidered. No doubt we will need to face, as Rosabeth Moss Kanter (1982) has well noted, the "dilemmas of managing participation." But if, in the final analysis and synthesis, we are prepared to see PM in its context, with its substantial strengths and its considerable difficulties, participative management continues to offer a promising range of powerful approaches to personal and organizational vitality.

Abstracts

Abdel-Halim, Ahmed A., and Rowland, Kendrith. "Some Personality Determinants of the Effects of Participation: A Further Investigation." *Personnel Psychology* 29 (Spring 1976): 41-45.

A replication is attempted of V.H. Vroom's 1960 study on participation in decision making, which showed more positive outcomes in effectiveness and satisfaction for egalitarian subordinates with high independence needs and less positive outcomes for authoritarian subordinates with low independence needs. In a large retail firm in the Midwest, measures of independence needs and authoritarianism were correlated with data derived from the Job Descriptive Index and supervisors' ratings. For the managers studied, Vroom's results were not replicated; this raises doubts as to the generality of the 1960 findings. This lack of generality may be accounted for by differences in the organizations studied and by variations in sample and method. Suggestions are presented for needed research.

13

Alutto, Joseph A., and Belasco, James A. "A Typology for Participation in Organization Decision Making." *Administrative Science Quarterly* 17 (March 1972): 117-125.

"Decisional participation" is defined as the difference between the number of decisions in which an individual wishes to participate and the number of decisions in which this individual actually participates. Subjects (n=454) are faculty in two separate school districts. Categorizing those responding in terms of a typology—*"deprivation," "equilibrium,"* and *"saturation"*—as relates to their participation in decision making, relevant differences are found in age, sex, teaching level, seniority, attitudes, and militancy. It is concluded, on the basis of evidence, that assumptions concerning the universal desirability of increased participation need to be modified.

Aplin, J.C., Jr.; Schoderbek, C.G.; and Schoderbek, P.P. "Tough-Minded Management by Objectives." *Human Resource Management* 18 (Summer 1979): 9-13.

MBO, by its very nature, calls for participation in various aspects of decision making by subordinates, in conjunction with their respective superiors. As an organizational tool it has passed through a period of considerable vogue; yet, in many instances, it has not proved successful. This lack of success may, in large measure, reflect an unjustified attribution of managerial know-how to subordinates by their superiors. It may be useful for managers to rethink their views of, and approaches to, MBO, assuming a more aggressive and tough-minded posture in implementation of such (participative) programs.

Bartlem, Carleton S., and Locke, Edwin A. "The Coch and French Study: A Critique and Reinterpretation." *Human Relations* 34 (July 1981): 555-556.

Traditionally, it has been proposed that a reduction of resistance to change is a likely outcome of participation in decision making. A 1948 field experiment conducted by Coch and French has become a much-cited classic in this connection. A reinterpretation of data, however, raises

Note: Special appreciation goes to Mahesh Gupta and Elsie Gum, respectively, for highly effective bibliographic and word processing assistance.

some questions concerning the conclusions usually drawn. Specifically, a number of associated but extraneous factors may have been responsible for the initially reported results, which pointed to the superiority of the combined experimental groups over the control group. These complicating factors include:

1. The manner in which the job changes were explained
2. Procedures used in the conduct of the time studies used as criteria
3. The amount of additional training given
4. Differences in the amount of work available
5. Differences in group size

Several of these factors may have combined effects to yield the results as originally published. Further, failure to find differences between *indirect* and *direct* participants in Group I raises some additional questions as to a participation interpretation. Instead, the critical factor may have been perceived fairness of pay rates and, more fundamentally, organizational trust.

14

Bartunek, Jean M. "Participation Training, Agreement, and Teacher Participation in Decision Making." *Group & Organization Studies* 5 (December 1980): 491-504.

This study notes differences among teachers in the desire to participate in decision making (specified by an agreement between teachers and principals), and examines the effects of participation training. Positive effects of such training are shown, with those who had received training preferring participation, especially when they anticipated that there would be a high level of agreement.

Bartunek, Jean M., and Keys, Christopher B. "Participation in School Decision Making." *Urban Education* 14 (April 1979): 52-75.

While this paper focuses on participation in decision making in school settings, its scope is generic and broadly relevant. A historical overview of the "participation" concept in organization theory is presented, and applications in schools are considered. Two examples of participation fostered by organization development are discussed, respectively, in a junior high school and in a parochial school system. Contingency approaches to participation are called for.

Bistline, Susan. "Participative Management." *Association Management* 32 (August 1980): 95-101.

It is essential that both managers and employees have clear expectations regarding any participative management program that may be instituted. Participative management is *not* equally applicable in all organization types, nor for all individuals. Under favorable circumstances participation may result in: (1) better decisions; (2) higher productivity; (3) improved morale and job satisfaction; (4) reduced tardiness, turnover, and absenteeism; and (5) better communication and resolution of conflict. Methods used to implement participative management may range in complexity from simple suggestion programs to pervasive changes in top-to-bottom management structure.

Bloomberg, Seth Allan. "Participatory Management: Toward a Science of Correctional Management." *Criminology* 15 (August 1977): 149-164.

In prison settings, participatory management calls for restructuring of decision-making processes, with increased responsibility assigned to prison inmates. Inmate subculture is an obstacle in this connection. However, participatory management may serve to counteract the negative effects of this subculture by the development of purposeful coalitions among staff and inmates.

Bragg, J.E., and Andrews, I.R. "Participative Decision Making: An Experimental Study in a Hospital." *Journal of Applied Behavioral Science* 9 (November-December 1973): 727-735.

In this experimental study, participative decision making was introduced into a hospital sub-system where several situational factors favored the success of such a program. Over the 18-month period of the study, records of 28 meetings were analyzed. Of the 147 employee suggestions, 11 involved hours of work and working conditions, 90 had to do with work flow (process and methods), 44 related to minor equipment modifications, and 2 were concerned with safety. In the experimental group, improvement in attitudes and decline in absence rates were observed. Performance differences between the experimental and comparison groups were statistically and practically significant.

15

Cooper, Michael R., and Wood, Michael T. "Effects of Member Participation and Commitment in Group Decision Making on Influence, Satisfaction, and Decision Riskiness." *Journal of Applied Psychology* 59 (April 1974): 127-134.

In an experiment in participation in structured decision tasks, conducted with 120 psychology students, perceived influence and satisfaction were greatest when the subject participated fully, rather than partially, in the task. A sense of impact, that is, perceived influence, was greatest when the subjects affirmed commitment to the outcome, but satisfaction proved to be greatest when no such commitment was required.

Dachler, Peter H., and Wilpert, Bernhard. "Conceptual Dimensions and Boundaries of Participation in Organizations: A Critical Evaluation." *Administrative Science Quarterly* 23 (March 1978): 1-39.

A conceptual framework is presented as the basis for analysis of participation in decision making. Four dimensions and their interrelationship are considered: (1) *contextual boundaries*, including characteristics of society, other relevant organizations, the focal organization, groups within the organization, and individuals; (2) *values, assumptions, and goals of implementers*, including issues such as democratic theory, and productivity and efficiency orientation; (3) *properties of participation*, including formal-informal aspects, direct-indirect aspects, access to decision, decision content, importance and complexity, and social range; and (4) *outcomes*, at individual, group, organizational, and societal levels.

DeVries, David L., and Snyder, John P. "Faculty Participation in Departmental Decision Making." *Organizational Behavior & Human Performance* 11 (April 1974): 235-249.

In a study of faculty participation in departmental decision making (n=387 faculty members in 46 departments), it is shown that factors associated with values of the individual correlate significantly with measures of participation. To a lesser degree, environmental factors also are shown to relate to these outcome measures, but the individual value variables provide the greater explanatory power.

Driscoll, James W. "Trust and Participation in Organizational Decision Making as Predictors of Satisfaction." *Academy of Management Journal* 2 (March 1978): 44-56.

Organizational trust—as indicated by potential participants' views of decision makers in the hierarchy—is shown to be of major importance in predicting the participants' levels of satisfaction. *Congruence* between desired and perceived participation best predicts satisfaction with participation in decision making.

Dudek, D.H. "Multiple Management." *(S.A.M.) Advanced Management Journal* 44 (Spring 1979): 26-31.

Developed by McCormick during the Great Depression, multiple management is a technique that can fulfill the demands of both management and employees. It is a form of participative management that allows managers from all divisions to work together on management boards, to solve problems, and to share ideas concerning new opportunities. Companies recognize that this provides a way for study and implementation of fresh ideas. At the same time, the procedure increases morale by giving employees a greater sense of involvement. By recognizing the relationship between employee development and company growth, multiple-management boards achieve both.

Geiger, Theodore. "The Movement for Industrial Democracy in Western Europe." *Challenge* 22 (May-June 1979): 14-21.

In Western Europe, industrial democracy, involving codetermination and worker participation in management, calls for alterations in organizational structure, decision-making techniques, and enterprise ownership in the market sector. Management's and owners' freedom in private enterprise decision making are reduced; trade unions and workers assume additional powers. Such power shifts appear at the levels of shop floor, boardroom, and stockholders' meetings. Industrial democracy at the shop level generally is implemented by establishment of works councils with worker representation. Boardroom arrangements typically provide for the presence of worker representatives at board meetings. Industrial democracy at the stockholders' meeting level has not yet been fully realized in any country. Known as "worker asset-information," principal proposals (1979) are the Meidner Plan (Sweden) and the Draft Law (Netherlands). Industrial democracy heightens centralized control in the economy, while reducing operation of market forces.

Glass, J.J. "Citizen Participation in Planning: The Relationship between Objectives and Techniques." *Journal of the American Planning Association* 45 (April 1979): 180-189.

In the context of citizen participation in urban planning, it is stressed that in each instance the *goals* of the participation program need to be clearly specified at the outset. Such goals may include (1) information exchange, (2) education, (3) support building, (4) supplemental decision making, and (5) obtaining representation inputs. Four participative techniques are discussed, including (1) neighborhood meetings, (2) citizen advisory committees, (3) group process, and (4) the citizen survey.

Greiner, L.E., and Schein, E. "The Paradox of Managing a Project-Oriented Matrix: Establishing Coherence within Chaos." *Sloan Management Review* 22 (Winter 1981): 17-22.

Matrix organization, involving coordinated effort in multidisciplinary teams, necessarily calls for distribution of authority and responsibility and thus involves various forms of participation. Various aspects of design and implementation of matrix structures are considered, and emergent problems are highlighted.

Hill, Thomas E., and Schmitt, Neal. "Individual Differences in Leadership Decision Making." *Organizational Behavior & Human Performance* 19 (August 1977): 353-367.

This investigation evaluates an abbreviated methodology for the study of Vroom and Yetton's (1973) normative model, including the issue of individual differences in participative decision making. With graduate-level management students serving as subjects, results indicate that the abbreviated methodology yields results substantially similar to those obtained by Vroom and Yetton. Much depends on the situation, but individual differences also have impact.

Jacob, Philip, and Ahn, Chungsi. "Around the World on the Automated Line." *Wharton Magazine* 3 (Spring 1979): 64-67.

A comprehensive inquiry, conducted in 15 countries, examined reasons why certain workers seek to influence decisions affecting their work while others do not choose to do so. The study found that: (1) while there are differences among workers in different countries, the broader economic environment—socialist or capitalist—seems to have little impact in this connection (a sense of having sufficient "clout" in determining working conditions is more important than economic ideology); (2) the influence of management on worker participation depends primarily on the effectiveness and power of the local trade unions; (3) when social conditions support a sense of individual potency and strength, a higher number of activists is found than when the opposite is the case (this occurs in otherwise contrasting sociopolitical and economic systems); and (4) the degree of "automatedness" does not appear to be strongly linked to participation in decision making.

James, Lawrence R., et al. "Correlates of Psychological Influence: An Illustration of the Psychological Climate Approach to Work-Environment Perceptions." *Personnel Psychology* 32 (Autumn 1979): 563-588.

In contrasting high-technology jobs (n=126) and low-technology jobs (n=205), the correlates of subordinates' perceptions of their psychological influence on supervisors' decisions are studied. It is found—noting the influence of the *psychological climate* characterizing the work environment—that the perceptions of influence are related significantly to *situational* attributes (such as supervisors' behavior), *individual characteristics*, and *interactions between person and situation*. The results suggest that how people cognitively process information affects their views of the influence that may be derived from participation in decision making.

Koch, James L., and Fox, Colin L. "The Industrial Relations Setting, Organizational Forces, and the Form and Content of Worker Participation." *Academy of Management Review* 3 (July 1978): 572-583.

A variety of forces co-act in industrial relations settings and in various organizational environments to influence the nature and direction of worker participation. Especially salient forces include:

- values
- the sociopolitical climate
- economic conditions
- bargaining structures
- organizational size
- organizational centralization
- organizational technology

In their unique combination, as illustrated by examples relating to several Western nations, these factors are critical in furthering or restraining worker participation.

Kolodny, H.F. "Evolution to a Matrix Organization." *Academy of Management Review* 4 (October 1979): 543-551.

18

While most matrix organizations are devised on the basis of prior traditional organization forms, matrix systems call for substantially different managerial styles and behaviors. Opportunities must be provided for the *organic step-by-step unfolding of patterns of development* that are consonant with the newly created matrix requirements.

Kolodny, H.F. "Managing in a Matrix." *Business Horizons* 24 (March-April 1981): 17-24.

It is noted that matrix organization involves participation in decision making by persons at different levels of responsibility and expertise, including the determination and implementation of operational decisions by employees at lower managerial levels. To effectively implement matrix organization, behavioral changes at a range of managerial levels—calling for time and effort commitments by all concerned—are required.

Likert, Rensis, and Fisher, M.S. "MBGO: Putting Some Team Spirit into MBO." *Personnel* 54 (January-February 1977): 40-47.

Management by objectives (MBO), as is well known, is a procedure in which subordinates participate with their superiors in developing objectives and in allocation of resources required for timely attainment of these objectives. Here it is suggested that, on an individual basis, such efforts on occasion may lead individuals to strive for their own particular goals at the expense of others. In turn, it is possible to create a procedure of management by group objectives (MBGO), in which managers and their subordinates act in teams throughout the objectives setting, implementation, and evaluation process.

Long, Richard J. "The Effects of Formal Employee Participation in Ownership and Decision Making on Perceived and Desired Patterns of Organizational Influence: A Longitudinal Study." *Human Relations* 34 (October 1981): 847-876.

In an electronics firm that converted to partial employee ownership, questionnaires were administered to affected employees as follows: seven months prior to the purchase, seven months thereafter, and following eighteen months of employee ownership. It was found that little change took place in:
- —perceived participation at each decision level,
- —desires for participation
- —distribution of control and influence

However, employees continued to support the participation mechanisms as instituted.

Lowin, Aaron. "Participative Decision Making: A Model, Literature Critique, and Prescriptions for Research." *Organizational Behavior & Human Performance* 3 (February 1968): 68-106.

A model of participative decision making in organizations is developed. The proposed framework places emphasis on conditions of equilibrium and social change associated with this process and its outcomes. Attitudes are viewed as a major mediating variable, affecting nature and consequences of participative decision making.

An experimental participative decision-making program is analyzed, and it is pointed out that research in this field may profit by explicit consideration of various mediating variables, avoiding formulation of questions in terms of simple cause-and-effect relationships, as often has been the case. Such change in strategy of inquiry may prove more productive than many conventional research approaches.

The literature on participative decision making to date (1968) is summarized and critically reviewed.

McConkey, Dale D. "Participative Management: What It Really Means in Practice." *Business Horizons* 23 (October 1980): 66-73.

Participative management is reconsidered in terms of a modified definition and a number of associated aspects. The definition may be paraphrased as follows: "Participative management is a decentralized team approach, giving managers latitude as regards determination and conduct of their jobs, in the framework of organizational requirements." Aspects of participative management implied by this definition include the following:
- responsibility
- authority
- accountability
- decision-making
- planning
- supervision
- communication and feedback
- managing, as such

Before attempting to institute participative management approaches, it is necessary that a clear assessment be made of the then-existing management style and of the organization's readiness to move in new directions.

McDaniel, Reuben R., Jr., and Ashmos, Donde P. "Participatory Management: An Executive Alternative for Human Service Organizations." *Human Resource Management* 19 (Spring 1980): 14-18.

Under conditions of high organizational complexity, participatory management constitutes a particularly appropriate management response, especially (1) if indicators of complexity are realistically assessed, and (2) if possible areas of difficulty in implementation of participatory management are carefully taken into account. Indicators of organizational complexity include:
—increased size
—complex goal negotiation systems
—levels of technology
—turbulent task environments
—nonroutine decision making
—high levels of uncertainty

Possible areas of difficulty in implementation are the following:
- —limitations in needed expertise at the task level
- —difficulties in coordination of task responsibilities
- —excessively narrow management approaches in evaluation of employee performance
- —overdependence on specific personnel
- —excessively diverse views of organization personnel concerning prevailing complexity and requirements for certainty

McKelvey, Bill, and Kilmann, Ralph H. "Organization Design: A Participative Multivariate Approach." *Administrative Science Quarterly* 20 (March 1975): 24-36.

By means of a procedure calling for direct inputs by organization members concerning their preferences for association, an organization (in this instance, a university faculty) was nominally redesigned. It was the purpose of this redesign effort to increase the organization's ability to respond more appropriately to changing environments by development of more cohesive and effective subunits. In turn, the subunits were to be in a better position to negotiate their objectives and to create suitable internal and external integrative devices, directed toward flexible and purposeful response.

McMahon, Anne M., and Camilleri, Santo F. "Organizational Structure and Voluntary Participation in Collective-Good Decisions." *American Sociological Review* 40 (October 1975): 616-644.

In an experimental study, based on a specified conceptual model, voluntary participation in activities intended to attain the "collective-good" of group members is examined. Organizational factors—not necessarily dependent on interpersonal processes—determine the efficacy by which the collective-good is attained. Degree of centralization of the authority system as such and the relevant participation rates affect outcomes. A conceptualization of an authority structure is proposed that is configurational rather than unidimensional, and ways to alter centralization are discussed.

Main, Jeremy. "Westinghouse's Cultural Revolution." *Fortune*, 15 June 1981, pp. 74-93.

Stimulated by managerial and decision-making styles recently identified with industrial organization in Japan (for example, "Theory Z"), the construction group at Westinghouse redesigned its management system, adapting concepts implemented in the Orient to American conditions. Participative management teams have been formed, and increasing numbers of decisions are reached by consensus. However, results are not always positive. While it is concluded that labor-management relationships have improved, substantial amounts of time are consumed by steps required to implement the system. Specific benefits have included recasting of various internal business systems, with anticipated major financial savings and massive changes in personnel utilization, especially in secretarial arrangements. Managers appear to be the most enthusiastic regarding the experiment, while blue-collar reaction ranges from quite cool to fairly warm. On balance, improvement in productivity is predicted.

Miller, Jon. "Decision Making and Organizational Effectiveness: Participation and Perceptions." *Sociology of Work and Occupations* 7 (February 1980): 55-79.

This inquiry, based on responses of 161 employees of a white-collar organization, concludes that differences in *organizational position* need to be taken into account in the assessment of the consequences of participation. The inquiry discovered that being allowed to participate is related to perceptions of effectiveness by subordinates. However, no such relationship is perceived by superordinates, that is, by superiors in hierarchy position. Indeed, the latter view centralization as an important determinant of effectiveness. These findings put into doubt some conventional assertions concerning the general benefits of participation in decision making.

Moran, Robert T. "Japanese Participative Management—or How Rinji Seido Can Work for You." *Advanced Management Journal* 44 (Summer 1979): 14-22.

Comparisons are presented between practices in major sectors of Japanese industry and the United States. It is concluded that because of cultural differences between the two countries, many Japanese management practices cannot be transferred to the United States. Japanese industry is characterized as emphasizing harmony, lifetime employment, promotion by seniority, and decentralized decision-making processes. U.S. industry tends to place stress on individualistic and directly competitive approaches, and on hierarchic decision making. While simple practice transfer from Japan to the United States is not indicated, one notes the sense of pride, personal worth, and familial identification with the enterprise that is widely prevalent in Japan. Management requests for worker input on policy change and on other issues of significant company concern, as in Japan, may be constructively applied in the U.S. situation.

Mulder, Mark, and Wilke, Henk. "Participation and Power Equalization." *Organizational Behavior & Human Performance* 5 (September 1970): 430-448.

Belief that participation in decision making will result in power equalization between "haves" and "have-nots" is criticized. Experiments are designed to test two hypotheses: (1) a higher degree of expert power (availability of relevant information) of Other will result in more effective influence by Other on Subject than a lower degree of expert power; (2) the higher the degree of expert power possessed by Other, and the greater the extent of Subject's participation with Other in the decision-making process, the greater Other's effective influence on Subject. Experimental findings strongly support these hypotheses. It is observed that members' perception of participation in the decision-making process suffices to raise the levels of satisfaction and involvement. The issue of "democratization" is considered.

Naor, Jacob. "Planning by Consensus: A Participative Approach to Planning." *Advanced Management* 43 (Autumn 1978): 40-47.

Participatory planning, with consensus as an objective, increases purposeful joint effort among management levels. While in conventional situations, corporate goals are stated at the top management level, with those at lower levels in the hierarchy seeking to formulate suitably responsive plans, planning by consensus provides opportunities for implementation of the planning process at the divisional level. Resulting plans are reviewed by other organizational units, including but not confined to, top management. A consensual overall long-range plan is developed. Problems in the introduction of this approach are discussed.

Neider, Linda L. "An Experimental Field Investigation Utilizing an Expectancy Theory View of Participation." *Organizational Behavior & Human Performance* 16 (December 1980): 425-442.

In a study based on a field experiment conducted in a family-owned chain of western New York retail stores, several hypotheses derived from an expectancy theory approach to participation are tested. As hypothesized, productivity and effort levels increased in the "experimental" store, in which both discussion groups on job-related issues and an incentive program to reward high hourly sales levels were instituted. No corresponding increases appeared under "other" or "control" conditions. By way of further support for the experimentally instituted participative approach, its subsequent application in what initially had served as the "control" store likewise brought about the anticipated positive results in productivity and effort levels.

22

Nightingale, Donald V. "Participation in Decision Making: An Examination of Style and Structure and Their Effects on Member Outcomes." *Human Relations* 34 (December 1981): 1119-1133.

Both formal decision-making structure and informal supervisory style variously incorporating or facilitating participation in decision making, are relevant in affecting outcomes for organization members, such as their levels of satisfaction.

For 1,000 organization members, in matched samples of 10 formally participative and 10 conventionally hierarchic organizations, *both* style and structure are found to have significant effects on member outcomes. Style, however, has a more potent effect than structure.

As expected, participative/supportive supervisory styles tend to be found in greater measure in formally participative organizations than in their hierarchic counterparts, and outcomes emerge as more positive in the former kinds of organizations than in the latter.

Further, supervisory style is likely to be more participative/supportive in organizations in which rank-and-file employees are given the opportunity to participate directly in decision making, as contrasted with organizations in which participation is indirect, as by means of forms of representation.

Norton, Steven D. "Employee-Centered Management Participation in Decision Making and Satisfaction with Work Itself." *Psychological Reports* 38 (April 1976): 391-398.

Focusing on satisfaction with work itself in a study of 120 management-level personnel of a large corporation, it was found that such work satisfaction is positively correlated with employee-centered management and with participation in decision making. However, these correlations were found to be lower than those between satisfaction and positive views of the work environment.

Ouchi, William G. "Theory Z Corporations: Straddling the U.S. and Japanese Molds." *Industry Week*, May 1981, pp. 48-50.

In an article-length statement of *Theory Z*, the author reviews aspects of Japanese management (Type J styles) and American management (Type A styles), and proposes that these styles are not necessarily culture bound. The author notes that Japanese management is based on shared reliance of objectives and procedures communicated through a common culture, and on symbols and rituals affirming underlying values. In Japanese management, participatory decision making proceeds by involving in the decision-making process all those likely to be affected by the decision. In contrast, the American management approach often assigns principal decision determination to not more than 8 to 10 people, upon discussion of alternatives among themselves. Rapid turnover in American companies tends to lead to formality and distance, impeding collective work styles. Type Z organizations, having characteristics of both A and J management styles, *are* found in the United States. They often acquire reputations for developing young people into effective senior managers.

"Participative Management Is Not New at McCormick Where Subordinates' Opinions Shake Things Up." *Data Management* 19 (October 1981): 42-43.

Participative management has been in use at McCormick & Company (Baltimore, Maryland) since 1932. Junior and middle-level managers are involved in this program. Boards of these lower-level managers meet regularly to consider issues of current and anticipated relevance and to transmit suggestions and ideas to top management for final determination. It has been found (on the basis of informal evidence) that communications between management levels increase, that the boards serve as useful management training settings, and that, particularly for data processing personnel, attrition and job switching are apparently effectively reduced by this participatory procedure.

Peters, T.J. "Beyond the Matrix Organization." *Business Horizons* 22 (October 1979): 15-27.

Following World War II, many organizations tended to change structure, from functional to divisional to matrix. Matrix organization often has not proved to be as effective as hoped. Other forms need to be considered. One alternative approach takes account of the competing organizational and environmental demands that initially generated interest in matrix, but recognizes realistic achievable limits. This emerging approach is based on the following four principles: (1) manage necessary routine; (2) learn to avoid pitfalls of "systems management"; (3) be responsive to limits resulting from the organization's past; and (4) never stop "reorganizing."

Rosen, B., and Jerdee, T.H. "Effects of Decision Performance on Managerial Willingness to Use Participation." *Academy of Management Journal* 21 (December 1978): 722-725.

In an analysis of management determination of optimum levels of employee involvement in decision making, it is concluded that managers are more willing to proceed with participative approaches when the decisions at stake can be implemented on a trial rather than on a permanent basis.

Rowen, T.D.; Howell, C.D.; and Gigliotti, J.A. "The Pros and Cons of Matrix Management." *Administrative Management* 41 (December 1980): 22-24.

Organizations are developing "dual responsibility" structures to cope with complex realities. Matrix management as an approach to organization design is considered from a number of perspectives, and illustrative cases in specific companies are examined. It is noted that effective construction of matrix organization needs to consider the impact of culture and business strategy. Examples at General Motors, Digital, General Electric, and ITT are cited.

Schuler, Randall S. "A Role and Expectancy Perception Model of Participation in Decision Making." *Academy of Management Journal* 23 (June 1980): 331-340.

Individual and organizational factors have an impact on the effectiveness of participation in decision making. Role and expectancy perceptions are influenced by organizational and individual conditions, such as organizational structure, task design, employee ability, and supervisory span. A role and expectancy perception model of participation in decision making is tested by means of a questionnaire study of 382 employees at three organization levels in a large manufacturing company, and of 429 employees in a large public utility. The data suggest that the role and expectancy perception model constitutes a useful approach in analysis of participation in decision making, satisfaction, and performance relationships. However, role conflict and ambiguity tend to reduce the effectiveness of participative decision making.

24

Smith, H. R. "A Sociobiological Look at Matrix." *Academy of Management Review* 3 (October 1978): 922-926.

Matrix organization is viewed in the context of human social/biological processes. It is suggested that the initial Generation I matrix designs overestimated human capacity for dealing with ambiguity and novelty, but that Generation II matrix approaches increasingly take account of these social/biological limitations of matrix personnel. With this perspective, it becomes possible to develop increasingly well-functioning matrix systems.

Stearns, Mary. "What's It All About, Alpha?" *Data Management* 19 (October 1981): 50.

This report, citing Rosener and Schwartz (1980),* notes that women are more likely than men to employ participative methods in the solution process. In turn, there was evidence that the women's solutions were superior to those presented by the men. Men are shown to choose hierarchic rather than participative forms.
  Alpha, associated with men, is based on analytical and rational thinking, win-lose logic, and hierarchic organization. *Beta*, associated with women, is based on intuitive thinking, cooperation, and adaptive/participative organization.
  Joint effort between Alpha and Beta styles tends to bring about optimal solutions, and development of a suitable balance between these styles constitutes a key consideration in the design of effective leadership.
  In Japan, males are more inclined to behave in a Beta manner, without fear of disapproval by their peers or superiors. In the United States, with such disapproval more prevalent, it is important that women in organizations not permit Alpha to squelch Beta.

Steers, Richard M. "Individual Differences in Participative Decision Making." *Human Relations* 30 (September 1977): 837-847.

This study examines the effect of several individual difference factors which relate to subordinates' participation in decision making. Females are found to be more participative than males, and such sex differences often affect the relationship to other personality variables. The ability to identify those specific individual characteristics most closely associated with

*See Recommended Reading

various aspects of decision-making behavior should assist in the development of more precise predictive models of the decision-making process. Vroom and Yetton's hypothesis, that the situation plays a greater role than do individual differences in the determination of allowed participation, is examined.

Thompson, Robert G. "Participative Management: A Way of Life?" *Business & Economic Review* 28 (October 1981): 3-9.

Prominent among the many current philosophies and practices designed to improve productivity is participative management. This approach appears to be on the way to becoming a "way of life" in the United States. Participative management calls for mental and emotional involvement by subordinates, motivates contributions, stimulates creative thinking, and encourages people to accept responsibility. Participative management may be applied in both the public and the private sectors. While participative management is not a panacea, it is a tool that can be used successfully to develop employee satisfaction.

25

Trist, Eric. "Collaboration in Work Settings: A Personal Perspective." *Journal of Applied Behavioral Science* 13 (July-August-September 1977): 268-278.

In modern society it becomes important to build organizations, especially work organizations, that are based on participation rather than on hierarchy. Organizations need to be transformed, to serve not only their own formal objectives but also the needs of their members and of the larger community. Bureaucracies develop in disturbed-reactive environments. New forms of organization emerge in present-day turbulent social environments. In such organizations, collaboration and intuitive and creative approaches are required to deal with uncertainty and with increased complexity. Autonomous work groups, various innovative plant designs, and continuous adaptive planning processes are illustrative of these evolving organization forms.

White, Kenneth J. "The Scanlon Plan: Causes and Correlates of Success." *Academy of Management Journal* 22 (June 1979): 292-312.

The Scanlon Plan, a well-established procedure for improving the effectiveness of organizations, is based on a formal participation program, coupled with a financial bonus arrangement. A study was conducted to identify factors associated with Scanlon Plan success. The research was implemented in 23 companies with present or past Scanlon Plan experience. Scanlon Plan success was found to be positively related to the average level of participation in decision making, as reported by employees; to the number of years of company experience with the Scanlon Plan; to management attitudes (especially the CEO's); and to the expected level of success. Company size was *not* a good predictor of SP success.

Wright, N.H., Jr. "Matrix Management: A Primer for the Administrative Manager." *Management Review* 68 (April 1979): 58-61.

Various forms of matrix organization are shown to face specific sets of difficulty and to yield specific benefits. It is possible to develop effective centralization, cost efficiency, flexibility in manpower utilization, and responsive planning and control. However, balance of power, functional project organization, authority relationships, and overall standards must be carefully assessed at every stage of the matrix to assure long-term effectiveness.

Recommended Reading

Abdel-Halim, Ahmed A., and Rowland, Kendrith. "Some Personality Determinants of the Effects of Participation: A Further Investigation." *Personnel Psychology* 29 (Spring 1976): 41-45.

Abrahamsson, B. "Bureaucracy or Participation—Logic of Organization." *Administrative Science Quarterly* 24 (1979): 143-144.

Allport, Gordon W. "The Psychology of Participation." *Psychological Review* 53 (May 1945): 117-132.

Alutto, Joseph A., and Belasco, James A. "A Typology for Participation in Organization Decision Making." *Administrative Science Quarterly* 17 (March 1972): 117-125.

Aplin, J.C., Jr.; Schoderbek, C.G.; and Schoderbek, P.P. "Tough-Minded Management by Objectives." *Human Resource Management* 18 (Summer 1979): 9-13.

Appelbaum, Steven H. "Human Resource Development: A Foundation for Participative Leadership." *Personnel Administrator* 24 (March 1979): 50-56.

Argyris, Chris. *Personality and Organization*. New York: Harper & Brothers, 1957.

Bartlem, Carleton S., and Locke, Edwin A. "The Coch and French Study: A Critique and Reinterpretation." *Human Relations* 34 (July 1981): 555-556.

Bartolke, Klaus, et al. "Workers' Participation and the Distribution of Control as Perceived by Members of Ten German Companies." *Administrative Science Quarterly* 37 (September 1982): 380-397.

Bartunek, Jean M. "Participation Training, Agreement, and Teacher Participation in Decision Making." *Group & Organization Studies* 5 (December 1980): 491-504.

Bartunek, Jean M., and Keys, Christopher B. "Participation in School Decision Making." *Urban Education* 14 (April 1979): 52-75.

Bass, Bernard M. *Stogdill's Handbook of Leadership*. New York: Free Press, 1981.

Bistline, Susan. "Participative Management." *Association Management* 32 (August 1980): 95-101.

Bloomberg, Seth Allan. "Participatory Management: Toward a Science of Correctional Management." *Criminology* 15 (August 1977): 149-164.

Bourdon, R.D. "A Basic Model for Employee Participation." *Training & Development Journal* 34 (April 1980): 24-29.

Bragg, J.E., and Andrews, I.R. "Participative Decision Making: An Experimental Study in a Hospital." *Journal of Applied Behavioral Science* 9 (November-December 1973): 727-735.

Brownell, Peter. "Participative Management: The State of the Art." *Wharton Magazine* 7 (Fall 1982): 38-43.

Burck, C.G. "Working Smarter." *Fortune*, 15 June 1981, pp. 68-73.

Cooper, Michael R., and Wood, Michael T. "Effects of Member Participation and Commitment in Group Decision Making on Influence, Satisfaction, and Decision Riskiness." *Journal of Applied Psychology* 59 (April 1974): 127-134.

Dachler, Peter H., and Wilpert, Bernhard. "Conceptual Dimensions and Boundaries of Participation in Organizations: A Critical Evaluation." *Administrative Science Quarterly* 23 (March 1978): 1-39.

DeVries, David L., and Snyder, John P. "Faculty Participation in Departmental Decision Making." *Organizational Behavior & Human Performance* 11 (April 1974): 235-249.

Davis, S.M., and Lawrence, P.R. "Problems of Matrix Organizations." *Harvard Business Review* 56 (May-June 1978): 131-142.

Dickson, John W. "Participation: A Remedy for Work Alienation." *International Review of Applied Psychology* 30 (January 1981): 87-101.

Donnelly, John F. "Participative Management at Work." An HBR interview. *Harvard Business Review* 55 (January-February 1977): 117-127.

Dowling, W.F. "Consensus Management at Graphic Controls." *Organizational Dynamics* 5 (Winter 1977): 23-47.

Drake, Matthias C. "Quaker Consensus: Helping Learners Understand and Participate in the Quaker Way of Reaching Group Decision." *Dissertation Abstracts International* 34 (May 1974): 6931-A.

Driscoll, James W. "Trust and Participation in Organizational Decision Making as Predictors of Satisfaction." *Academy of Management Journal* 2 (March 1978): 44-56.

Drucker, P.E. "Managing in Turbulent Times—Management Loses Its Power Base." *Industry Week*, 12 May 1980, pp. 42-48.

Dudek, D.H. "Multiple Management." *(S.A.M.) Advanced Management Journal* 44 (Spring 1979): 26-31.

Duncan, R. "What Is the Right Organization Structure?" *Organizational Dynamics* 7 (Winter 1979): 59-80.

Foy, N., and Casey, D. "Perils of Participation." *Management Today*, July 1977, pp. 47-49.

Geiger, Theodore. "The Movement for Industrial Democracy in Western Europe." *Challenge* 22 (May-June 1979): 14-21.

Glass, J.J. "Citizen Participation in Planning: The Relationship between Objectives and Techniques." *Journal of the American Planning Association* 45 (April 1979): 180-189.

Greiner, L.E., and Schein, E. "The Paradox of Managing a Project-Oriented Matrix: Establishing Coherence within Chaos." *Sloan Management Review* 22 (Winter 1981): 17-22.

Hader, John J., and Lindeman, Eduard C. *Dynamic Social Research*. New York: Harcourt Brace, 1933.

Handy, C. "Management by Consent." *Management Today*, February 1977, pp. 68-72.

Hill, R.E. "Managing Interpersonal Conflict in Project Teams." *Sloan Management Review* 18 (Winter 1977): 45-61.

Hill, Thomas E., and Schmitt, Neal. "Individual Differences in Leadership Decision Making." *Organizational Behavior & Human Performance* 19 (August 1977): 353-367.

Jacob, Philip, and Ahn, Chungsi. "Around the World on the Automated Line." *Wharton Magazine* 3 (Spring 1979): 64-67.

James, Lawrence R., et al. "Correlates of Psychological Influence: An Illustration of the Psychological Climate Approach to Work-Environment Perceptions." *Personnel Psychology* 32 (Autumn 1979): 563-588.

Janis, Irving L. "Decisionmaking under Stress." In *Handbook of Stress*, by Leo Goldberger and Shlomo Breznitz. New York: Free Press, 1982.

Kanter, Rosabeth Moss. "Dilemmas of Managing Participation." *Organizational Dynamics* 10 (Summer 1982): 5-27.

Kavcic, Bogdan, and Tannenbaum, Arnold S. "A Longitudinal Study of the Distribution of Control in Yugoslav Organizations." *Human Relations* (UK) 34 (1981): 397-417.

Kilmann, Ralph H., and Herden, Richard P. "Towards a Systemic Methodology for Evaluating the Impact of Interventions on Organizational Effectiveness." *The Academy of Management Review* 1 (July 1976): 87-98.

Koch, James L., and Fox, Colin L. "The Industrial Relations Setting, Organizational Forces, and the Form and Content of Worker Participation." *Academy of Management Review* 3 (July 1978): 572-583.

Kolodny, H.F. "Evolution to a Matrix Organization." *Academy of Management Review* 4 (October 1979): 543-551.

———. "Managing in a Matrix." *Business Horizons* 24 (March-April 1981): 17-24.

———. "Matrix Organization Designs and New Product Success." *Research Management* 6 (Summer 1977): 43-61.

"Labor: A Try at Steel-Mill Harmony." *Business Week*. Industrial Edition (No. 2694). 29 June 1981, pp. 132-136.

Lawrence, P.R.; Kolodny, H.F.; and Davis, S.M. "The Human Side of Matrix." *Organizational Dynamics* 6 (Summer 1977): 43-61.

Lederer, Victor. "Decision Making: Should Employees Get in on the Act?" *Administrative Management* 39 (September 1978): 51-52.

Lewin, Kurt; Lippitt, Ronald; and White, Robert K. "Patterns of Aggressive Behavior in Experimentally Created 'Social Climates.' " *Journal of Social Psychology* 10 (1939): 271-299.

Likert, Rensis. *New Patterns of Management*. New York: McGraw-Hill, 1961.

Likert, Rensis, and Fisher, M.S. "MBGO: Putting Some Team Spirit into MBO." *Personnel* 54 (January-February 1977): 40-47.

Lin, W.T. "Corporate Planning and Budgeting: An Integrated Approach." *Managerial Planning* 27 (May-June 1979): 29-33.

Locke, E.A., and Schweiger, D.M. "Participation in Decision Making: One More Look." In *Research in Organizational Behavior*, edited by B.M. Staw and L.L. Cummings. Greenwich, Conn.: JAI Press, 1979.

London, M. "Effects of Shared Information and Participation on Group Process and Outcome." *Journal of Applied Psychology* 60 (October 1975): 537-543.

Long, Richard J. "The Effects of Formal Employee Participation in Ownership and Decision Making on Perceived and Desired Patterns of Organizational Influence: A Longitudinal Study." *Human Relations* 34 (October 1981): 847-876.

Lowin, Aaron. "Participative Decision Making: A Model, Literature Critique, and Prescriptions for Research." *Organizational Behavior & Human Performance* 3 (February 1968): 68-106.

McConkey, Dale D. "Participative Management: What It Really Means in Practice." *Business Horizons* 23 (October 1980): 66-73.

McConkie, M.L. "A Clarification of the Goal Setting and Appraisal Processes in MBO." *Academy of Management Review* 4 (January 1979): 29-40.

McDaniel, Reuben R., Jr., and Ashmos, Donde P. "Participatory Management: An Executive Alternative for Human Service Organizations." *Human Resource Management* 19 (Spring 1980): 14-18.

McGregor, Douglas. *The Human Side of Enterprise*. New York: McGraw-Hill, 1960.

McKelvey, Bill, and Kilmann, Ralph H. "Organization Design: A Participative Multivariate Approach." *Administrative Science Quarterly* 20 (March 1975): 24-36.

McMahon, Anne M., and Camilleri, Santo F. "Organizational Structure and Voluntary Participation in Collective-Good Decisions." *American Sociological Review* 40 (October 1975): 616-644.

Main, Jeremy. "Westinghouse's Cultural Revolution." *Fortune*, 15 June 1981, pp. 74-93.

Marrow, Alfred J.; Bowers, David G.; and Seashore, Stanley E. *Management by Participation.* New York: Harper & Row, 1967.

Miller, Jon. "Decision Making and Organizational Effectiveness: Participation and Perceptions." *Sociology of Work and Occupations* 7 (February 1980): 55-79.

Moran, Robert T. "Japanese Participative Management—or How Rinji Seido Can Work for You." *Advanced Management Journal* 44 (Summer 1979): 14-22.

Mulder, Mark, and Wilke, Henk. "Participation and Power Equalization." *Organizational Behavior & Human Performance* 5 (September 1970): 430-448.

Naor, Jacob. "Planning by Consensus: A Participative Approach to Planning." *Advanced Management* 43 (Autumn 1978): 40-47.

Neider, Linda L. "An Experimental Field Investigation Utilizing an Expectancy Theory View of Participation." *Organizational Behavior & Human Performance* 16 (December 1980): 425-442.

Nightingale, Donald V. "Participation in Decision Making: An Examination of Style and Structure and Their Effects on Member Outcomes." *Human Relations* 34 (December 1981): 1119-1133.

————. "The Formally Participative Organization." *Industrial Relations* 18 (Fall 1979): 310-321.

Norrgren, Flemming. "Assessing Managers' Beliefs about Participation." *Reports from the Department of Applied Psychology*, vol. 6. Goteborg, Sweden: University of Goteborg, 1981a.

————. "Managers' Beliefs, Behavioral Intentions, and Evaluations with Respect to Participation." *Reports from the Department of Applied Psychology*, vol. 6. Goteborg, Sweden: University of Goteborg, 1981b.

Norton, Steven D. "Employee-Centered Management Participation in Decision Making and Satisfaction with Work Itself." *Psychological Reports* 38 (April 1976): 391-398.

Ouchi, William G. "Theory Z Corporations: Straddling the U.S. and Japanese Molds." *Industry Week*, 4 May 1981, pp. 48-50.

————. *Theory Z: How American Business Can Meet the Japanese Challenge.* Reading, Mass.: Addison-Wesley, 1981.

"Participative Management Is Not New at McCormick Where Subordinates' Opinions Shake Things Up." *Data Management* 19 (October 1981): 42-43.

Pascale, Richard Tanner, and Athos, Anthony G. *The Art of Japanese Management—Applications for American Executives.* New York: Simon and Schuster, 1981.

Peters, T.J. "Beyond the Matrix Organization." *Business Horizons* 22 (October 1979): 15-27.

Raghavan, S.V. "Workers' Participation in BHEL." *Vikalpa* (English language periodical, published in India) 3 (July 1978): 163-166.

Rosen, B., and Jerdee, T.H. "Effects of Decision Performance on Managerial Willingness to Use Participation." *Academy of Management Journal* 21 (December 1978): 722-725.

Rosener, L., and Schwartz, P. "Women, Leadership and the 1980's." In *New Leadership in the Public Interest* (New York: NOW Legal Defense and Education Fund, 1981). Available from the publisher.

Rothschild-Whitt, Joyce. "Conditions Facilitating Participatory-Democratic Organizations." *Sociological Inquiry* 46 (1976): 75-86.

Rowen, T.D.; Howell, C.D.; and Gigliotti, J.A. "The Pros and Cons of Matrix Management." *Administrative Management* 41 (December 1980): 22-24.

Russel, R.; Hochner, A.; and Perry, S.E. "Participation, Influence, and Worker-Ownership." *Industrial Relations* 18 (Fall 1979): 330-341.

Sashkin, Marshall. "Changing towards Participative Management Approaches: A Model and Methods." *The Academy of Management Review* 1 (July 1976): 75-86.

Schuler, Randall S. "A Role and Expectancy Perception Model of Participation in Decision Making." *Academy of Management Journal* 23 (June 1980): 331-340.

Segovis, James C., and Bhagat, Rabi S. "Participation Revisited." *Small Group Behavior* 12 (August 1981): 299-327.

Shipper, F.M. "Anticipatory Management—The Key to the Eighties." *Management World* 9 (January 1980): 15-28.

Smith, H.R. "A Sociobiological Look at Matrix." *Academy of Management Review* 3 (October 1978): 922-926.

Stearns, Mary. "What's It All About, Alpha?" *Data Management* 19 (October 1981): 50.

Steers, Richard M. "Individual Differences in Participative Decision Making." *Human Relations* 30 (September 1977): 837-847.

Tannenbaum, Robert, and Massarik, Fred. "Participation by Subordinates." In *Leadership and Organization*, by Robert Tannenbaum, Robert Weschler, and Fred Massarik, pp. 88-100. New York: McGraw-Hill 1961. (Adapted from an earlier article in the *Canadian Journal of Economics and Political Science*, 1950.)

Tannenbaum, Robert, and Schmidt, Warren H. "How to Choose a Leadership Pattern." *Harvard Business Review* 51 (May-June 1973): 162-172 (originally published in the *Harvard Business Review*, 1958).

Tavernier, G. " 'Awakening a Sleeping Giant. . .': Ford's Employe Involvement Program." *Management Review* 70 (June 1981): 15-20.

32

Thompson, Robert G. "Participative Management: A Way of Life?" *Business & Economic Review* 28 (October 1981): 3-9.

Trist, Eric. "Collaboration in Work Settings: A Personal Perspective." *Journal of Applied Behavioral Science* 13 (July-August-September 1977): 268-278.

Turney, J.R., and Cohen, S.L. "Participative Management: What Is the Right Level?" *Management Review* 69 (October 1980): 66-69.

Vroom, Victor H. *Some Personality Determinants of the Effects of Participation*. Englewood Cliffs, N.J.: Prentice-Hall, 1960.

————. *Work and Motivation*. New York: Wiley, 1964.

Vroom, Victor H., and Yetton, Philip W. *Leadership and Decision Making*. Pittsburgh, Pa.: University of Pittsburgh Press, 1973.

Warr, Peter, and Wall, Toby. *Work & Well-Being*. Middlesex, England: Penguin Books, 1975.

Weihrich, H. "TAMBO: A Team Approach to MBO." *University of Michigan Review* 31 (May 1979): 12-17.

White, Kenneth J. "The Scanlon Plan: Causes and Correlates of Success." *Academy of Management Journal* 22 (June 1979): 292-312.

Williams, Ervin, ed. *Participative Management: Concepts, Theory, and Implementation*. Atlanta, Ga.: College of Business Administration, Georgia State University, 1976.

Wolff, M.F. "The Joy (and Woe) of Matrix." *Research Management* 23 (March 1980): 10-12.

Wright, N.H., Jr. "Matrix Management: A Primer for the Administrative Manager." *Management Review* 68 (April 1979): 58-61.

————. "Matrix Management—Fortifying the Organization Structure." *Management World* 9 (May 1980): 24-26.

Additional Reading

Appley, Dee G., and Winder, Alvin E. "An Evolving Definition of Collaboration and Some Implications for the World of Work." *The Journal of Applied Behavioral Science* 13 (July-August-September 1977): 279-291.

Bartunek, Jean M. "Decision Characteristics, Organization Development Training and Teacher Participation in Decision Making." *Dissertation Abstracts International* 37 (April 1977): 5429.

Bass, Bernard M. "Amount of Participation, Coalescence, and Profitability of Decision-Making Discussions." *Journal of Abnormal and Social Psychology* 67 (July 1963): 92-94.

Bluestone, Irving. "Worker Participation in Decision Making." *The Humanist* 33 (September-October 1973): 11-15.

Boddy, D. "Participation in Decision Making in the Health Services." *Journal of Advanced Nursing* 3 (July 1978): 349-358.

Cascino, A.E. "How One Company 'Adapted' Matrix Management in a Crisis." *Management Review* 68 (November 1979): 57-61.

Chadwick, David. "Participation through Joint Consultation." *Employee Relations* 1 (No. 3, 1979): 9-12.

Cherniss, Cary, and Egnatios, Edward. "Participation in Decision Making by Staff in Community Mental Health Programs." *American Journal of Community Psychology* 6 (April 1978): 171-190.

Child, J. "Participation, Organization, and Social Cohesion." *Human Relations* 29 (May 1976): 429-451.

Coleman, P.G. "Using a Matrix Organization." *Journal of Systems Management* 30 (December 1979): 36-37.

Cooper, Michael R. "Satisfaction, Perceived Influence, and Decision Riskiness: The Effects of Participation and Commitment in Decision-Making Groups." *Dissertation Abstracts International* 33 (October 1972): 1835.

Crowe, Donald O. "The Elementary Principal's Orientation toward Teacher Participation in Decision Making." *Dissertation Abstracts International* 34 (August 1973): 526-527.

Elden, J.M. "Political Efficacy at Work—the Connection between More Autonomous Forms of Workplace Organization and a More Participatory Politics." *American Political Science Review* 75 (1981): 43-58.

Falconer, M. "Power Versus Participation: The New Leadership Style." *Leadership* 1 (December 1980): 18-23. Special pullout publication within *Association Management* 32 (December 1980). *Leadership* is published annually in this form.

Greenberg, Edward S. "The Consequences of Worker Participation: A Clarification of the Theoretical Literature." *Social Science Quarterly* 56 (September 1975): 191-209.

Harvey, D. "The Lusty Growth of CMG." *Director* 31 (October 1978): 76-78.

"Have Large Organizations Outgrown the One Boss-One Worker Management System?" *Association Management* 30 (October 1978): 92.

Heller, F.A., et al. "Longitudinal Study in Participative Decision Making." *Human Relations* 30 (1977): 567-587.

Hollon, C.J., and Gemmill, G.R. "Comparison of Female and Male Professors on Participation in Decision Making, Job-Related Tension, Job Involvement, and Job Satisfaction." *Educational Administration Quarterly* 12 (Winter 1976): 80-93.

Jago, Arthur G., and Vroom, Victor H. "An Evaluation of Two Alternatives to the Vroom/ Yetton Normative Model." *Academy of Management Journal* 23 (June 1980): 347-355.

Jenkins, T. "Participative Management." *Management World* 10 (May 1981): 8-10.

Johnson, Dale A. "A Study of Relationships between Participation in Decision Making, Job Satisfaction, and Selected Personality Variables of Secondary School Principals." *Dissertation Abstracts* 29 (1969): 3377-3378.

Johnson, R.J. "Problem Resolution and Imposition of Change through a Participative Group Effort." *Journal of Management Studies* 11 (1974): 129-142.

Kovach, K.A.; Sands, B.F.; and Brooks, W.W. "Is Codetermination a Workable Idea for U.S. Labor-Management Relations?" *MSU Business Topics* 28 (Winter 1980): 49-55.

"Labor: A Try at Steel-Mill Harmony." *Business Week* (Industrial Edition), 28 June 1981, pp. 132+.

London, Manuel. "The Effects of Participation and Information Group Process and Outcome." *Dissertation Abstracts International* 35 (November 1974): 2476-2477.

Looper, C.E. "Framework for Managing a Multiunit Organization." *Magazine of Bank Administration* 55 (July 1979): 43-46.

Manz, C.C., and Sims, H.P. "Self-Management as a Substitute for Leadership: A Social Learning Theory Perspective." *Academy of Management Review* 5 (July 1980): 361-367.

Marlow, H. "Participation: A Practical Approach for the Smaller Company." *The Director* 29 (June 1977): 60-62.

Mohrman, A.M.; Cooke, R.A.; and Mohrman, S.A. "Participation in Decision Making—Multidimensional Perspective." *Educational Administration Quarterly* 14 (Winter 1978): 13-29.

Muhs, William F. "Worker Participation in the Progressive Era: An Assessment by Harrington Emerson." *Academy of Management Review* 7 (January 1982): 99-102.

Nelder, Linda L. "An Experimental Field Investigation of the Motivational Processes Involved in Participative Decision Making." *Dissertation Abstracts International* 40 (March 1980): 4547.

Nigro, Lloyd G., and Bellone, Carl J. "Participative Management: Making It Work." *Bureaucrat* 8 (Winter 1979-1980): 34-39.

Peach, Larry E. "Perceptions of Participation in Decision Making and Satisfaction with Decisions Made in the Knox County School System." *Dissertation Abstracts International* 39 (February 1979): 4635-4636.

Pollay, Richard W.; Taylor, Ronald N.; and Thompson, Mark. "A Model of Horizontal Power Sharing and Participation in University Decision-Making." *Journal of Higher Education* 47 (March-April 1976): 141-157.

Rose, Ed. "Generalized Self-Management: The Position of Henri Lefebvre." *Human Relations* 31 (July 1978): 617-630.

Ruh, R.A.; White, J.K.; and Wood, R.R. "Job Involvement, Values, Personal Background, Participation in Decision Making, and Job Attitudes." *Academy of Management Journal* 18 (1975): 300-312.

Russell, R.; Hochner, A.; and Perry, S.E. "Participation, Influence, and Worker-Ownership." *Industrial Relations* 18 (Fall 1979): 330-341.

Simmons, J. "Participatory Management at the World Bank." *Training & Development Journal* 34 (March 1980): 50-54.

Singer, J.N. "Participative Decision Making about Work—An Overdue Look at Variables Which Mediate Its Effects." *Sociology of Work and Occupations* 1 (November 1974): 347-371.

Styskal, Richard A. "Power and Commitment in Organizations: A Test of the Participation Thesis." *Social Forces* 58 (March 1980): 925-943.

Swierczek, F.W. "Collaborative Intervention and Participation in Organizational Change." *Group & Organization Studies* 5 (December 1980): 438-451.

Tsaklanganos, A.A. "Peers, Persuasion, and Horizontal Management." *Management Accounting* 60 (August 1978): 33-37.

Tytler, K. "Making Matrix Management Work—and When and Why It's Worth the Effort." *Training* 15 (October 1978): 78-82.

Wall, W.C., Jr. "The Two-Tier Matrix Organization in Project Management." *Defense Systems Management Review* 1 (Autumn 1978): 37-46.

Warner, W. Keith, and Highlander, James S. "The Relationship between Size of Organization and Membership Participation." *Rural Sociology* 29 (March 1964): 30-39.

Weigel, R.H., and Cook, S.W. "Participation in Decision Making—Determinant of Interpersonal Attraction in Cooperating Interracial Groups." *International Journal of Group Tensions* 5 (December 1975): 179-195.

Wood, M.B. "Organization of Successful Participative Management in a Health-Sciences Library." *Bulletin of the Medical Library Association* 65 (April 1977): 216-223.

Wood, Michael T. "Participation, Influence and Satisfaction in Group Decision Making." *Journal of Vocational Behavior* 2 (October 1972): 389-399.

Yien, Shan-Pang. "Employee Participation in Organizational Decision Making and Acceptance of Planned Change." *Dissertation Abstracts International* 31 (May 1971): 6166.

38

Additional Reading

(INTERNATIONAL)

Bacot, E. "France: Participation French Style." *The Director* (UK) 30 (January 1978): 31.

Berisch, G.K., and Obradovic, J. "Participation and Influence in Yugoslav Self-Management." *Industrial Relations* 18 (Fall 1979): 322-329.

Bunker, B.B., and Alban, B. "Industrial Democracy." *Group and Organization Studies* 4 (September 1979): 265-272.

Chadwell, P.A. "Worker Influence in European Company Policy." *Directors & Boards* 2 (Summer 1977): 26.

Cooper, C.L. "Developing Organizational Life: Participation at Work." *Leadership & Organization Development Journal* 1 (1980): 15-19.

Dickson, John W. "Participation as a Means of Organizational Control." *Journal of Management Studies* (UK) 18 (April 1981): 159-176.

Dufty, N.F., and Williams, J.G. "Participation in Decision Making." *Journal of Educational Administration* (Australia) 17 (1979): 30-38.

El-Namaki, M.S. "Matrix Organization: A Possible Solution to the Organizational Problems of the Tanzanian Export Sector." *International Review of Administrative Sciences* (Belgium) 44 (1978): 277-282.

Gerstenfield, A., and Sumiyoshi, K. "The Management of Innovation in Japan—Seven Forces That Make the Difference." *Research Management* 23 (January 1980): 30-34.

Heller, Frank A. "Realities of Participation." *Management Today* (UK) (March 1978): 74-77.

Heller, Frank A., and Wilpert, Bernard. "Limits to Participative Leadership: Task, Structure and Skill as Contingencies—A German-British Comparison." *European Journal of Social Psychology* (Netherlands) 7 (1977): 61-84.

Hethy, L., and Mako, C. "Workers' Direct Participation in Decisions in Hungarian Factories." *Personnel Review* (UK) 7 (1978): 18-24.

Kannappan, Subbiah, and Krishnan, V.N. "Participative Management in India: Utopia or Snare?" *The Annals of the American Academy of Political and Social Science* 431 (May 1977): 95-102.

Laurent, A. "Matrix Organizations and Latin Cultures." *International Studies of Management & Organization* 10 (Winter 1980): 101-114.

Lind, O. "Employee Participation in Sweden." *Employee Relations* 1 (1979): 11-16.

Loveridge, Ray. "What Is Participation? A Review of the Literature and Some Methodological Problems." *British Journal of Industrial Relations* (UK) 18 (November 1980): 297-317.

Maruta, V. "The Management of Innovation in Japan—The Tetsuri Way." *Research Management* 23 (January 1980): 39-41.

Nielsen, R.P. "How Inclusive Should a Consulting Report Be in a Participative Decision-Making Situation." *Personnel Review* (UK) 9 (July 1980): 54-55.

Parrot, T., et al. "Matrix Management: A Case Study." *Optimum* 10 (1979): 64-73.

"Participation: Formal Rules, Influence, and Involvement." *Industrial Relations* 18 (Fall 1979): 273-294.

Rosenberg, R., and Rosenstein, E. "Operationalising Workers' Participation: A Comparison of U.S. and Yugoslav Models." *Industrial Relations Journal* (UK) 12 (March-April 1981): 46-52.

Szal, R.J. "Popular Participation, Employment and the Fulfillment of Basic Needs." *International Labour Review* 18 (January-February 1979): 27-38.

Veljko, Rus, et al. "Participative Decision Making: A Comparative Study." *Industrial Relations* 18 (Fall 1979): 295-309.

Warner, M. "Participative Decision Making in a Consultative Committee Context." *Relations Industrielles/Industrial Relations* (Canada) 29 (No. 2, 1974): 272-284.

A WORK IN AMERICA POLICY STUDY

PRODUCTIVITY THROUGH WORK INNOVATIONS
directed by **Jerome M. Rosow**, President & **Robert Zager**, Vice President for Policy Studies and Technical Assistance, both of Work in America Institute

It has often been proven that work innovations increase productivity. Indeed, evidence dating back 40 years demonstrates that well-designed programs employing workers more productively have achieved productivity growth rates far above the norm.

Now **Productivity Through Work Innovations** shows how to improve productivity in the 80s and 90s by giving employees more say in decisions affecting their jobs. This Policy Study puts innovative programs like job enrichment, labor-management committees, gain-sharing plans, relatively autonomous work teams and more in the context of today's workplace, showing how to use them to increase productivity.

In addition, the Study points out the prospects and pitfalls you may encounter in establishing these innovative programs: the costs and benefits of introducing, diffusing and institutionalizing such innovations. It also examines the effectiveness of these strategies for all types of personnel, from blue- and white-collar workers to professional, managerial and technical staff.

Productivity Through Work Innovations is the complete guide to increasing productivity in the 80s and beyond.

176 pp.	**1982**	**029545 2**	**hardcover**	**$15.00**
Also available: Executive Summary		029546 0	softcover	$ 6.50

CURRENT BOOKS

THE INNOVATIVE ORGANIZATION: Productivity Programs in Action
edited by Robert Zager & Michael P. Rosow, both of the
Work in America Institute

A companion volume to the Policy Study **Productivity Through Work Innovations**, this important new book containing 13 case studies looks at key organizations — such as General Motors, Citibank and Ford Motor Company — that have used work innovations to encourage employee participation in decision making and to increase productivity. Each distinguished contributor (usually someone closely related to the project) describes the program and its objectives; shows how it was launched, implemented, diffused and institutionalized; and discusses its successes and failures.

300 pp.	**1982**	**029547 9**	**hardcover**	**$27.50**

INDUSTRIAL BEHAVIOR MODIFICATION: A Management Handbook
edited by Richard M. O'Brien, Hofstra University, Alyce M. Dickinson, State of N.Y. Office of Court Administration & Michael P. Rosow, Work in America Institute

Industrial Behavior Modification is an original and ground-breaking work that translates the principles of behavior modification and applied behavioral analysis into practical techniques for industrial psychologists and managers. Illustrated with classic studies and new case material, this handbook shows how to motivate workers more effectively, increase productivity, build sales, evaluate performance, manage stress and improve the quality of working life.

Published by Pergamon Press in cooperation with the Work in America Institute.

480 pp.	**1982**	**025558 2**	**hardcover**	**$35.00**

Work in America Institute, Inc.

A nonprofit organization
founded to advance productivity
and the quality of working life

ISBN 0-08-029
ISSN 0149